How to Become Famous on Tik Tok

A Step-by-Step Guide for Beginners on How to Harness the Power of This New Hot Trend to Make Money, Gain Fame and grow Your Brand – TikTok 2020.

By

Martin Baldrön

Table of Contents

Part 1

Introduction

How TikTok has changed the social media game

TikTok was one of the most talked-about social media applications in recent times, and for both good and bad reasons has become a subject for discussion. TikTok is a social media app that allows users to generate short videos, from lip synchronization, comedies, talent videos, etc. to people who live under the rock. In 2017, ByteDance, the Chinese company, launched the app mainly for markets and regions outside China. TikTok is available on iOS as well as Android. TikTok has a worldwide 500 million active users, making it the 9th largest social network website in terms of other social networking sites including Facebook, Snapchat, Twitter and Pinterest. In Q1 2019 alone, TikTok had about 13.2 million new users in the United States, a rise of 181 percent year-over-year, or 2.8 times the 4.7 million installs that it had in Q1 2018. The development of the app has been primarily accredited in India. In Q1 19, the app was joined by an estimated 88.6 million people. This was 8.2 times more than in Q1 18 and mostly Android, whereby Google Play accounted for almost 99% of downloads.

TikTok: The Next Big Social Media App

Since its launch, the app has grown enormously. TikTok, now known as Douyin in China, was launched as A.me back in 2016. Douyin had about it. In just one year from the launch, 100 million users and 1 billion video views a day. It was only renamed TikTok in

September 2017 when it was launched internationally. However, TikTok's game changed when in Dec 2017 it acquired the popular Musical.ly video app. Once users of Musical.ly had shifted totally to TikTok, the real impact of TikTok began, particularly on the international market.

TikTok App

In 2018, TikTok recorded 600 million global downloads and became the world's fourth most downloaded app, with WhatsApp, Messenger, and Facebook. TikTok became the most downloaded app all year long and was popular in the world's top three mobile markets—China, the USA and India.

Let's talk about money now. TikTok's revenues in 2017 were $3.5 million, 42% from the US, 39 percent from China (and Chinese Android users are excluded). In 2017, byteDance, the parent company, had $2.5 billion in revenue, worth $75 billion, making it the most valued private start-up in the world that surpassed Uber. ByteDance raised $3 billion by SoftBank in October 2018.

What makes TikTok Special

Where are more applications like TikTok on the market (not the same), what makes TikTok stand out is that it is more fun to use? Its algorithms work in a way that users can watch binge. However, what makes the app most successful is that it is created and offers creators a wide range of opportunities.

TikTok App Screen

You can either lip-sync or play comedy drafts (TikTok created your comedy line), and you can also select songs, sound bites, visual effects, etc. Interestingly, the app allows you to work with anyone in the app to perform a "duet" by merely reacting to their video. This creates a split-screen and reactions to an endless line. And, because it wasn't enough, the app allows users to upload their sounds so that creators can lip-sync to the original sounds of other users. And top of the cherry, TikTok makes everything easy and extremely easy to use.

How TikTok is evolving an important marketing tool

TikTok has become essential to marketing and brand opportunities, as any social media app. The app focuses primarily on video and thus becomes a valuable tool, particularly for younger target audiences.

One of TikTok's most significant marketing opportunities is influencer marketing. From maquillage to fashion, tutorials to cooking and baking, TikTok has a large group of influencers in this area, so it is essential for brands to target products in particular. Some of these influencers of TikTok have millions of followers, and that is your specific target group.

Another important aspect of this application is the creation of your channel and the posting of original content. This keeps your entire contents under control, and you can post unique videos in accordance with your brand's wishes. However, it is essential to ensure that the content is suitable and viral for the tool.

For example, Chipotle, the popular US fast-food Mexico brand, posted videos of a tortilla-chip bowl with a guacao bowl in the background of the Adele song, "Like Someone." Since the bite of the sound had the audience of Adele singing the song, the video felt like nachos sing to the guac.

Comparison

It is harmless to say that virtually no apps on the market were exactly like TikTok during the rise of TikTok. Interestingly, Facebook launched in 2018, an iOS-like TikTok-like app called Lasso. Lasso has been developed to allow users to create short videos. Facebook, however, kept the launch very quiet, and the app saw no promotions. It was downloaded in Feb 2019 by only 70,000 U.S. users. But Lasso didn't see much traction or hype.

Nevertheless, the Facebook family tried again recently, with Instagram's launch of Reels. Instead of launching a completely new app for that purpose, however, Reels has been launched and replicates TikTok as a feature of the popular Instagram stories. The features of Reels are the same as TikTok, but the fact that it is an add-on to Instagram can work for the company because of the scale at which Instagram operates. This feature is only accessible in Brazil, and no news can be added to other markets.

Controversies

Like any popular social media application, TikTok saw it as a fair number of disputes. The Indian government sent a ruling banning the app in the country earlier this year. This has become a significant problem for the app as Indian users make up the majority of TikTok's user base. ByteDance also stated that the ban cost them $500,000 every day (€ 386,000), putting more than 250 jobs at risk. The app is being fired for illegal content, allowing' pornographic,' shady and paedophile content. The Indian government also cited issues such as child pornography exposure. Sadly, India saw three to four deaths as well as people filming TikTok videos. But the ban was ultimately lifted.

Another major issue with TikTok is the lax enforcement of age restrictions: in February 2019 the Federal Commerce Commission (FTC), in violation of the 1998 Children's Online Data Protection Act (COPPA, 1998), slapped the company with a record fine of US$ 5.7 million for illegally collecting user data from children under 13.

Although the app is growing massively, it is speculated that growth might die as it did in the past for vines. However, it is impossible to predict as the vineyards were only vaguely similar to TikTok. However, we know one thing for sure that the app will continue to grow and become popular in the future, despite the controversy and the negative air around this app. The fact that influencers, brands and celebrities use this app now also demonstrates that the app is here to stay.

How To Make Money on TikTok

Since it was released on iOS and Android in 2017, TikTok's video-sharing app has made huge strides in popularity. "Tok is the world's leading target for short-form mobile videos," she added. "The idea behind TikTok is to enable people to produce short videos with their smartphones easy and quickly, allowing everyone to be a creator of media. As of July 2019, over 500 million active monthly users are active and become one of the world's leading contenders in video creation.

Like all Internet-based trends, TikTok quickly raised the question: can you make money on this thing? The answer is yes, surely you can. While TikTok is not explicitly designed to monetize creators and deliver income flows, the app is highly commercial-friendly and creatively leverage the platform. TikTok does not share ad revenues with creators as of this writing (July 2019). Still, there are imminent rumours that this is about to change and that the app takes a more YouTube-like approach to enable successful creators to generate revenues from their videos directly.

In this section, I'll talk about how to make money from TikTok. There is no "magic formula" or "rich-fast scheme"; there is no secret technique that allows you to post a TikTok video every day and retire in a month to your Tuscan villa to travel around the Mediterranean by speedboats. If there were, I would use it, not tell you. Instead, I will talk about the fundamentals and give you suggestions for thinking about platform monetization, so you can decide how to proceed. Making money at TikTok is like making money elsewhere—work, creativity, luck and —most importantly—creating value so other people want to be part of what you do. You don't make money if you don't create value.

Method One: Be An "Influencer"

Being an "influencer" online is, in fact, a legitimate way of curbing your online presence, although in recent months the term "influencer" has received many bad terms. This is because it sometimes seems that every half-attractive youth decides to be an "influencer," purchases 50,000 fake followers on Instagram, and then seeks to convey the actual goods and services in exchange for reviews and exposure. However, it is tough to be influential and famous by merely affirming your influence and fame unless you are Kim Kardashian.

Authentic influencers are people who have an accurate organic follow-up of actual human beings who value and respect "the influencer" when discussing their field of expertise. There are many real influencers in the world, large and small in scale. Your friend, whom you trust implicitly in music—the person is an influencer, whether he has three other "fans" like you or three million. Food criticisms for primary (or even minor) newspapers are usually influential, as are film critics. Martha Stewart was once a powerful influencer on a bigger scale and still has a lot of influence. Oprah Winfrey was probably the most influential; the simple mention of a book on his show had sufficed to make him a bestseller of #1 and the author himself a media figure. Today the trend seems to be smaller, but still significantly affected people.

Notice something familiar to all the influencers I mentioned? With their opinions, they all add value.

You don't listen to your friend because she's got a cool website or because your friends told you she was excellent, you listen to her, so if she recommends an album, you know it's going to be good. Every time she opens her mouth, she saves you time and money, and that's why you pay attention to her.

Food critics and film reviewers are driving people away from crappy restaurants and bad movies and into good ones. You add value to the world by having an opinion that proves to be a usually trustworthy judge as to whether or not something is worth your time and money. Martha Stewart manufactures fantastic recipes and crafts that people can aspire to. Almost always Oprah Winfrey recommended books and authors, which were excellent.

So, while "influencers" are real and you might be one, you must be aware that if your opinion does not add value, you do nothing worthwhile on the line of influence. You will not gain or maintain, popularity other than through flukes of luck or manipulation. You have to say something useful.

When you have something worth saying, and real people pay attention to your views, then TikTok gives you a straightforward method to monetize your video appearance in the app. You recommend products and services that you genuinely use and think is right; those brands, shops, artists or anyone delighted to redeem your advocacy of their product or service. You need to have a massive and committed follow-up—a bunch of pretenders you've shot on Tinder just won't cut it. However, you can easily earn thousands or tens of thousands of dollars in a shot with a real influence to boost the product of someone else.

Please note that many influencers have found it challenging to accept brand deals and not tell their followers the deal. Although it slightly reduces the value of your opinion to many people, I think that you have to say, in the long run, that you accept such deals because the consequences of the agreement that is shown that you DIDN'T unveil is a massive scandal that will damage your reputation, which in the first place undermines the very thing that makes you an influence.

Method Two: Live Streaming

Live streaming on TikTok used to take place via the.ly live URL mainly aimed at the musical performance (whether it's lip-syncing or live). The current exchange rates vary over time, but the basic system is simple: TikTok users can buy "coins" via in-application purchases using real money. Then you can use your coins (and other derivative currencies) to advise creators of TikTok and necessarily give them little real money to thank them for creating good live content. It is generally not a fortune, but it can be an income stream, although you must take payment in the form of digital gifts rather than money; that is not too hard to translate into cold hard m TikTok spends 80 percent of the value of the tip on the person making the live stream, building his account (and not incidentally signing to brans that he or she is gaining influence).

Method Three: Promoting / Selling Your Own Ventures

This is probably the most realistic way to make money for most people via TikTok, without accumulating a large number of people and becoming a national influencer. The secret is to use TikTok as a completely free way to promote and sell your products or services or to promote your existing businesses. The great thing is that all (legal) business or service, be it nerdy, crafty, techy or crazy, can be.

For example, you may have a rafting service that takes people every summer on rafting trips along the Colorado River. Well, every raft trip you make can be videoed, and you can make 15 seconds clips to show how unbelievable fun people are. Post it on TikTok, together with a few promotional frames showing where you are and how you can contact, what you charge and when your next trip is. TikTok doesn't pay you for anything directly, but now your company makes thousands of dollars for referrals and new customers that you draw with your videos. Another example is someone that has the craft business—say you make cool glass sculptures with melted glass. (And, of course, you may put videos on your Facebook page, your YouTube channel etc.) You can make super-fast videos of How-I-It showing your techniques and how good you are at them, highlighting your best and most beautiful work and, incidentally, mention that you can also sell these sculptures on your website. You can not only sell products directly from your videos but also attract people who like your work, which TikTok covers for you instead of paying for the bandwidth.

Finally, in essence, you can advertise any business even if it doesn't work well for video. By placing a fun, funny, creative or musically great video you're going to draw attention–then you can pitch your product or service with a few frames at the end.

Method Four: Amazon Referral Links

You can make a lot of money from Amazon referral links if you do, but some people may feel confused with proposing you can do it at Tik Tok. How will you promote anything if your video and bio have no links? You cannot expect your viewers to write the link and then type it by hand in a browser, and even if they did, it might cost you your Amazon account! The rules of Amazon prevent any linked system that obscures or spoils them from telling where a particular link originated. You want your viewers to click and tap, not write down and retype. A manual link entry does that.

So how are we doing that?

Your bio is the first place for writing TikTok information. (You can add text to the videos, but the video itself is often distracted.) However, there are no links on your bio page, either–you can have text, but it can't be clicked/taped. Users can't even copy it and paste it later into a browser. So, what can you do? What can you do? You want to focus your bio on a short text string: a shortened URL to your affiliate marketing page if the primary URL is unworkable, uncatchy or only the single URL is short.

Chapter 1

How New Influencers Are Making Millions with The Platform (and why I'm here to tell you that ehm... wait let me post another video on Tik Tok)

TikTok is the fastest growing social media platform today. It was downloaded more than Snapchat, Instagram, Snapchat, and YouTube in 2018 alone. If you don't know it yet, it's time to check it out.

TikTok combines the Vine comedy, which is the famous six-second video app that ended its operation in the year 2017, and the Musical.ly app, which was rebranded and acquired by TikTok in August 2018 and purchased by ByteDance in 2017.

With over 1 billion downloads from the App Store and Google Play, TikTok offers influencers the opportunity to interact with more than 500 million users and to take advantage of the platform with their commitment.

Running an agency that is very focused on TikTok, and I'm a fan of the app myself, I tested some customer campaigns. I thought of how influencers can earn money, which works well on social media platforms such as Instagram and YouTube. I have selected four of my favorite ways to make a TikTok influence to earn money.

1. **Gifting**

A TikTok user can go live and interact with thousands of users directly by commenting and chatting. The viewer can donate coins, a virtual currency that can be purchased by everyone in the app using the fingerprint ID, or face recognition. Coins purchased by users can then be donated during a live session to the influencer.

Every registered user can easily verify updated prices by opening the app, by clicking on the' Privacy and Settings,' by clicking on' Wallet,' and then by clicking on' Recharge.' The smallest package in the USA is 99 cents per 100 currencies. Once the live feed is over, the influencer can collect 50% of the coins, turn them into diamonds and then withdraw the corresponding amount of the dollar. The remaining 50% is divided between TikTok and the App Store or Google Play, respectively.

2. Influencer Marketing

During the years, social media marketing has grown in popularity through platforms such as Instagram and YouTube. Influencers can promote their followers ' products or services and be compensated by a company. Users of TikTok can generate one or more short clips in their style to promote the products of a company. It can be comedic or informative based on the audience and decisions of the influencer. Compensations vary according to factors like the number of supporters, commitment rate, types of products or services being promoted, number of videos produced, industry, and geolocation.

One of the essential factors to identify is that the video must be original and felt natural without a hard-selling technique. Instead of a staged ad, users prefer funny and entertaining videos, especially on TikTok. Another factor is to ensure that the activation can quickly become viral to be shown on the page "For you" so that organic exposure is increased.

3. Merchandising

Content creators and influencers can benefit additionally from TikTok by designing and selling their commodities (the most profitable of clothing lines). To maximize profit, there must be an extensive follow-up and a sense of community for an influencer.

Given my personal experience with various social media outlets, notably YouTube, Instagram, and Twitch, the majority of supporters do not purchase promoted products based on product value alone (for example, quality of material), but rather support the influencers or join a common trend. The influence of building a personal brand is crucial if an influencer is to create an online character, a recognizable logo, and an approach to a particular niche market before customary merchandise can even be sold online.

4. Events and Brand Partnerships

Lastly, brands and corporations are also invited to participate as a special guest in events, music festivals, or conferences that will pay TikTok users to promote brands, perform on stage (dancing or singing) or meet supporters.

In this case, the earnings can also vary according to the influence of the TikTok user who requests the brand's activities before, during, or after the event and

if the brand offers anything besides the TikTok user-
for instance paying for the flight and the hotel.

In conclusion, TikTok is a relatively new social media
platform that grows rapidly not only in China but in
the US and Europe as well. Brands and users alike can
benefit from a business perspective. It's the right time
to jump on TikTok for business purposes before the
acquisition channel is saturated and more costly.

*Now that you know their secret, you can attract
followers to your Tik Tok account and also start
making money.*

TikTok is much harder than Instagram. It takes much
effort to post cool vids from picking a song to editing.
However, TikTok is on the verge, and video content is
very attractive. How do you make your video famous
on TikTok and drive more views? We found several
hacks about how to get followers on TikTok and
improve the content reach.

Everything You Need to Know About Marketing on TikTok

If you didn't live under a rock, you probably heard the
buzz over the TikTok social media app. And with its
user-friendly content viewed by millions of people
every day, it is easy to understand why TikTok ads
have become increasingly popular.

TikTok is a marketer's dream with the app attracting
500 million active users worldwide, but how do
TikTok publicity work? And is it even possible as a
small business to advertise on it?

We have you covered when you're curious about marketing on TikTok but don't know where to start. We researched, rolled through the videos, and compiled this helpful guide, which will give you the tools to understand TikTok ads, its user base, and its different functions and features.

Read more about TikTok's strange and marvelous world and how your business can become part of it.

What's the TikTok application?

TikTok is a social media application that allows users to create and view music or custom soundtracks of short videos. Perfect for widespread use, while users can passively browse TikTok—scrolling and viewing the content of other users without helping, the app also makes video creation extremely easy for users.

But, before we jump into the features of the application, you might wonder where TikTok came from —and its journey to global popularity is an interesting one for good reasons.

The app is owned by ByteMedia, which launched the Douyin app in September 2016. TikTok —using the same software as Douyin—was released a year later as Douyin's international counterpart. Not long after this, ByteMedia acquired the lip-syncing app Muscial.ly and quickly gained popularity, combining both apps in August 2018.

With such rapid growth, some creators from TikTok became wildly popular and attracted attention from outside. One user was even signed off the back of a viral post with a talent agency.

In September 2019, the NFL endorsed a multi-year alliance with TikTok users to share game highlights and material behind the scenes. Meanwhile, a mixture of leading individuals, groups, and outlets, including Will Smith, Gary Vaynerchuk, The Washington Post, and the Korean Boy Band, BTS, has also been developed as popular TikTok profiles.

Who is using TikTok?

So, who is watching all these creators of random content? Well, they are mostly under 30, especially those who belong to Gen Z—a huge 41% of TikTok users are 16-24 years of age. And with this age range having growing purchasing power, TikTok ads and advertising are all the more important to understand.

With all this in mind, how can firms use TikTok's power?

Having only been around in its present form since late 2018, the TikTok advertising world has been very early. Although there may be significant future changes, here are the current ways in which a brand can use the marketing app:

1. Creating a Profile

The most affordable way to get involved in TikTok marketing is to create a profile, produce content, and build an audience. There is, however, the fine art of making videos that not only promote your brand but attract viewers. Users who don't use the application to watch TikTok ads, so any brand that wants to participate should understand the content that's popular before starting an account.

2. Payment for Official TikTok Ads

That seems to be an obvious answer to TikTok ads, but at this time, this option is only available in some countries and is priced restrictively. Paid TikTik ads can be made in several different ways including

- Pre-roll ads: videos that start after users open the application
- In-feed ads: videos that appear as users scroll

Promoted Hashtags: videos encourage user entry using a custom Branded hashtag: A custom-made effect filter for video creators, similar to Snapchat and Instagram and featuring brand specifics.

3. Working with influencers

Working with a proven, relevant TikTok influence to promote your product is a pleasant intermediate step between spending thousands on TikTok ads and trying to make your content. This has all kinds of businesses, from established brands such as Elf Cosmetics and Petco to smaller firms wanting to promote a single product.

However, it isn't always easy to direct websites to traffic from these videos because you can't include clickable URLs in TikTok's video titles. In their video or bio-comment section, you can try to work around this by having influencers link to your store, but as you can imagine, this additional step reduces it.

4. Shoppable Videos on TikTok

You may have heard that TikTok offers whispers of shoppable videos. This is a brand new option, currently being tested by a few TikTok influencers and available for some time on TikTok's sister Douyin app. Together with Instagram's "Swipe Up" function and shopping posts, shoppable videos would enable users to attach a URL to their TikTok advertising videos so that users can be taken to their shop with a single touch.

While TikTok has confirmed that they are testing the feature, it has not confirmed when or whether it is delivered to a broader audience, so shoppable videos cannot currently be seen as a viable option. If this feature is released around the world, it will open TikTok to marketing influencers and make selling directly from your company profile easier.

Regardless of which TikTok advertising option you are interested in, you still need a relevant and smart ad to make a difference. With the majority of internet-aged TikTok users, they are very knowledgeable about the advertising and don't want to see anything openly. But this doesn't imply that they are against advertising— it just has to fit in.

So, what is the best way to advertise for brands in TikTok? Use the unique features and user culture of the app.

Using App Features

TikTok, users often base their content on trends, as opposed to social media sites such as Facebook or Twitter. It can change quickly–what is popular one week will not necessarily warm the next week–and the key is to jump on the trends as soon as possible. Also, reactionary content is highly rewarded, while the original content is appreciated. Here are a few of the different types of content that your TikTok marketing could consider.

Hashtag Challenges

A hashtag challenge is to set a specific task by one user and other TikTok users to try it and post the result with the corresponding hashtag. Any user can try and create a hashtag challenge, although it is not guaranteed whether others join and spread.

If brands pay for the hashtag challenges, they will promote their hashtags for a few days and will usually be accompanied by a microsite where users can buy TikTok's brand products. That's what Kroger did when they ran the Hashtag challenge #TransformUrDorm during the back to the school shopping season.

If your brand or product has a popular hashtag challenge, it could be an excellent opportunity to jump on the bandwagon and try some views. Make sure you browse other videos via the hashtag to get a sense of how you can interact.

Creating and reusing sounds

This may be the remains of TikTok's Musical origins, but the use of "sounds" in videos is a significant part of TikTok's work. Song snippets, speeches, TV, movie dialog, and random user comments may be included. The brilliant part is that if a sound is used in a video, it is stored on TikTok and then re-used by other creators.

A son that became popular at TikTok brought mega-stardom to some musicians, including Lil Nax X whose song "Old Twin Road" was first a hit at TikTok, before it was mainstreamed, remixed and recorded for 19 weeks, the longest in the history at the number one Billboard Hot 100.

Often sounds are used together with other features of TikTok, such as hashtag challenges, as seen in #yeehaw's challenge and dance challenges, as seen in the git up challenge below.

Dance Challenges

Given the popularity of TikTok music, dance challenges appear to be a no-brainer. They are spread by dancing to a specific song and by recreating it by others. The dance itself can be elaborate or elaborately recreated–or both.

Take, for example, the challenge of the Git Up, where people dance to the song of Blanco Brown with the same name. Though Brown or his team did not create the challenge, the work of TikTok user Harvey Bass, videos with the hashtag #thegitup received more than 157 million views. And the flow-on effect was Brown's song on Spotify with more than 127 million streams.

On the other side, you have the popularity of the "Chinese New Year" dance performed by the band Sales. The dance is exceptionally uncomplicated, leaving users in increasingly incredible ways to show their creativity. Like song Blanco, "Chinese New Year" has also had an enormous boost in Spotify streams.

Duets and Effects

TikTok has a wide variety of filters and special effects, which users can use in their videos. Duets are a popular style that enables users to take a video with them and record a complementary video. Often duets are used when other users try to replicate what the original TikTok user did, such as cooking and crafting. Or, it could serve as a cool or creative counterpart to the original video.

TikTok frequently updates its filters, and users always find new ways of using it. The split effect of nine cameras was recently popular when a creator used it in combination with the song "M. Sandman," the Chordettes song. Others soon jumped in the format with a tendency reaching its peak when a cat was shown, which led to many literal copycat videos.

All these features have a lot of potentials for brands to jump into and market on TikTok, whether you want to pay for it or use influencers yourself. Nevertheless, this list is not exhaustive, and since it is all so new, it is important to remember, there is no way to create the best TikTok commercials.

Find Your Groove with TikTok Ads

You can always browse TikTok to find what is popular and jump into any of these features and formats when you see a format, sound, or hashtag that you like. Since TikTok is such a place of creativity, TikTok marketing is the limit for the sky. And since it is still not quite clear what the best way to build TikTok ads is to start experimenting and testing anything that could work for brands with lower marketing budgets.

In particular, TikTok users want clever and fun videos, so it's only time before you get a new video if you hit these notes with the videos you create. However, do not expect it to be instant, while some users can only go viral from one video, most of them take multiple attempts before everything comes together. And the ease with which everyone can create content is one of the many factors that give TikTok a competitive advantage. With these statistics from TikTok in mind, you will be able to understand the new social media events better. These statistics also prove that TikTok is not a power to be taken lightly, whether you are a social media marketer or a social media user. It's time to take TikTok seriously.

How Brands Are Using Tiktok

According to the social media team in HubSpot, the social video application TikTok "leaks" with brand opportunities. With over 500 million monthly active users, the one-year-old platform, which allows users to make short, bending videos with special effects and musical overlays, booms, most of them young= adult.

While Gen-Z has begun to show its creative side with the platform, some brands are also starting to experiment. But since TikTok is still such a young app, many marketers might wonder, "Is it worth it?" This question is understandable since TikTok has only recently initiated an advertising process and brand hyper-linking capabilities.

However, the current big TikTok brands have done an excellent job of using it instead of generating traffic or leading information for brand awareness. They use it to reach younger audiences and show themselves a lighter side through funny videos, challenges, and other strategies that you would only see on the platform. As TikTok is so unusual, brands must be creative to get their audience's attention. This innovative and quick-paced app might not be a simple ad or sponsored influencer endorsement.

Although it is too early to develop a list of best practices around TikTok marketing, it is a great time to get inspired by brands that have thought out of the box and succeeded in the app.

In this section, we will discuss seven companies and organizations, which are already viral or successful in TikTok. We will also offer takeovers that are suitable for even smaller companies to build a scalable, fun, and creative strategy.

Chipotle

The popular Mexican restaurant chain, Chipotle, has more than 55,000 TikTok fans. You publish several posts using music, memoirs, and other menu items. Here are two examples: a video shows tortilla chips squeezed in a bowl of guac with the Adele song, "someone like you," overlaying the clip, to celebrate #oneyearofTikTok. Since Adele's audience sings back to her in the sound bite, it feels like the chips sing to the guacao.

This is a fun way to create a well-known piece in a video that shows menu items creatively.

In this video that is posted on National Avocado Day, Chipotle clicks a popular memorandum by posting, "TFW guac is free. Online / in app-only 7/31

#GuacDance Terms: chip.tl/avoday." This video was not just suited to the meme-friendly, but also a viral #GuacDance Challenge. In only one week, TikTok has become the most successful brand challenge ever.

Although the original video is a quite clear plug for free guacamole, TikTok felt that its contents were perfect because they were musical, stupid, and pop culture. This is a good example of how a brand can promote its product with a beloved song or reference.

Although it can be difficult to challenge a viral, post, or encourage one— especially if one of your products is involved— it can help your company spread awareness of your brand. It also enables you to engage excitingly with potential new fans.

People who didn't know much about the restaurant deals or menu could take part in the challenge, be involved, and indirectly learn about the brand. If you need a creative way to spread brand awareness quickly, it could be a great experiment to take a note from Chipotle and to start challenges on any social media platform.

NBA

The NBA account combines game highlights with inspiring quotes and music montages with a whopping 5,1 million fans.

Contrary to its Instagram channel, which focuses exclusively on basketball games and highlights, the TikTok posts from NBA show an organization's lighter side. For instance, they often post player videos that work dramatically in music, dance on the court, or team mascots ' adventures.

While you can expect the NBA to concentrate more seriously on statistics and matches, it uses the musical features of the app to lighten branding and make its athletes more related. While basketball still supports videos, they also fit with other funny or musical posts in TikTok feeds. When a brand or company shows a more personal side, the public may begin to talk to it a little bit more. Even if a viewer is not a basketball fan, if a funny or motivational video has been watched, they could still think of following NBA players or rooting certain teams.

In other business environments, it can have the same effect to make your brand more personal. For example, if the TikTok account in your restaurant posts funny videos of waiters, viewers may think there is a nice staff at the restaurant. That could make them want to eat because they think that they are having a fun waiter and positive vibes dining experience.

United Nations IFAD

If you think about the marketing of agriculture or government groups, your last place would be on the app like TikTok.

But with its fascinating account, the IFAD (International Fund for Agricultural Development) of the United Nations challenges that misinterpretation.

The group, which aims to combat world hunger by promoting rural farming, uses TikTok to make people more aware of its cause. While most of the reports on this list use humor to engage fans, the IFAD has taken an approach that includes informative posts and videos that encourage viewers to change the world.

The IFAD publishes high-quality short films of farmers worldwide in the more informative posts. This allows viewers to learn how farming works and why it can solve world hunger.

IFAD recently created the #danceforchange challenge. As part of the challenge, the organization, using the #danceforchange hashtag in captions, encouraged audiences to film themselves dancing.

This is a great example of how creative development can help you or your brand become aware of dryer issues, such as agriculture or world hunger. Although the organization seeks to disseminate knowledge about a serious subject, it uses beautifully shot videos, peppy music, and challenges to involve, motivate, and entertain audiences.

Taking into account IFAD's strategy could be helpful for companies or organizations, such as the public, legal, or financial industries that have a serious mission. It may feel inappropriate or unnatural to make funny videos on a tough subject.

You can make a more informative way, such as the FIDA, by filming short stories or by starting a challenge to learn something about your mission.

The Washington Post

The Washington Post was one of the earliest adopters of TikTok. Those who did not view their videos on other social networks, but followed them, might anticipate research or serious content. But the Washington Post actually works differently on TikTok.

Surprisingly, the journal actually uses its account to post videos and newsroom scripts behind the scenes. These videos fit the platform perfectly because they are funny, musical, and embrace some of the strangest special effects of TikTok.

The Washington Post shows how brands on a social platform can succeed by talking directly to their particular audience. The prestigious newspaper doesn't try to stand on a platform like that. Most people already know the publication and respect it. The marketers also don't try to post research videos that might be more interesting to older crowds.

The team instead adapts content to young spectators who want to laugh and enjoy themselves. And even if they post edgy content, it's not completely off-brand. Their posts are still nice, funny, and show you the true people behind hard journalism. Young spectators could see these cheeky videos and trust journalists because they look like narrative people. That's why fans may go to The Washington Post as a reliable news source if they want to read something they identify with written by sources.

Since the Post has a long history of groundbreaking, winning and intellectual journalism, this humble and comedic approach to social media can also attract young readers who wish to follow the news, but are concerned that newspaper content is too advanced or out of touch.

If your brand is in publishing, universities, or similar industries, it could be an interesting experiment to test a video strategy that shows your lighter side. It could reduce the intimidation of your content and brand and help you get attention from new audiences.

Guess

Guess has only 35,000 fans and only three posts, but the high-tech company is listed because it was the first to challenge TikTok. Shortly after the launch of the app, TikTok partnered with Guess for the challenge #InMyDenim that encouraged users to film in interesting places while wearing the new denim line. They also had to overlay "I am a mess" by Bebe Rexha. Though they did not do much video testing, Guess showed how a challenge on a highly visual platform like TikTok could quickly spread product-based awareness. A challenge such as this that shows directly clothing worn by real people can also encourage customers who could see and want to buy an outfit for themselves.

This is a strategy that other fashion companies or companies that sell visually interesting products could easily use. An e-commerce firm would like to sell a new line of spinning chairs, for example. It may launch a challenge called "# SpinnyChairChallenge," in which participants spin into a certain song in one of the chairs of the brand.

Individuals who watch these videos might want to discover more about a brand that began such a strange challenge, or they could watch the chairs and buy one for their office.

San Diego Zoo

Everyone once in a while loves a cute animal video. And the TikTok account in the San Diego Zoo takes pleasant advantage of this well-known fact.

The strategy of the zoo is simple: post videos of nice, funny animals. And it seems to work with over 50,000 fans. How could anyone, after seeing this lounging meerkat video not follow them?

This is not only attractive for penguin lovers, but it is also a great example of how two similar brands use TikTok functions to promote cross-promotion. This video could be seen by aquarium and zoo fans due to the zoo tagging strategy. Thus, zoos may become more interested in the aquarium and vice versa.

Sometimes your brand can fit perfectly with a new social media application. When that occurs, it can be necessary to get on and experiment. The San Diego Zoo is an excellent example of a brand that quickly identifies and fully embraces a fitting platform. This can be much more profitable at the end of the day than spending valuable time on platforms that are meaningless for your industry or fan base.

NBC's Stay Tuned

Originally, NBC's Stay Tuned was a Snapchat news show produced by NBC aimed at Gen-Z. Following success on that platform, the network began to create TikTok content. The account with almost one million fans offers a mix of videos behind the scenes and fast news pieces that touch on odd events and pop culture.

Like the Washington Post, Stay Tuned creates much lighter content than the usual journalistic work of NBC News. Their videos are speedy, well-edited, and focused on stories that may appear more interesting for younger audiences in the app if they are reporting stories. While Stay Tuned has been successful in Snapchat, they do not repurpose content or put similar content on both channels. The news team customizes each content to the app on which it is published.

Stay tuned demonstrate how creating unique content for different platforms can give you significant gains in brand awareness and engagement, while small companies may need to repurpose contents to save resources. Because they have done so well in curating and tailored news stories for emerging platforms, Stay Tuned's strategy may help publishers, entertainers, bloggers, or academics looking to post on different platforms news, studies, or other exciting topics.

Tips for Brands on TikTok

While it might be hard to find your content virally like more prominent brands, TikTok could be an excellent tool for syncing with younger audiences. Tips for brands on TikTok. And as the app is so new, you can experiment with any strategy that you want to see if it works. If you believe TikTok might soon or in the future be part of your marketing strategy, it is a good time now to push your competitors forward by downloading the app and investigating what similar brands or potential audiences do there.

If you're eager to pursue TikTok, here are some tips we can get from looking at brands that have done well in the app. Show your company's different side. The app is a hub for humor and creativity. Using a more personal tone or an approach behind the scenes could make your firm more relational or reliable to potential customers.

Don't be frightened of experimenting. As already mentioned, the app is unbelievably new. Unlike platforms like Facebook and LinkedIn, the rules for what works and what doesn't exist as many norms or best practices. If you think something could be interesting or funny, try it and see if you have any questions, comments, or shares.

Join your audience. There are plenty of ways to communicate between challenges, duets, likes, comments, and shares with other TikTok users— even if you do not know them. Try to create videos, challenges, or duets to interact with others. The more you engage with individuals, the more your fan base can grow like other platforms.

Even if you don't want TikTok now, we strongly recommend that you check out the app. While it may be too niche for you right now, its branded videos may help your Brainstorm content ideas for your existing social platforms or provide you with an insight into how other companies experiment with new platforms.

Chapter 2

Why You Must Incorporate TikTok NOW in Your Marketing Strategy (Works for Every Industry)

You must enjoy the information on Tik Tok until now, but one thing is that we love tested and tested as marketers. We walk the road well, lacking time, budget, or the chance to pursue strategies that will not ensure you achieve results.

But from time to time, something is coming to disturb your methods. And whether you jump in when it's new or wait until it's tested, that's up to you. Often through your competitors.

TikTok is this disruptor

As part of the social media analysis by Talkwalker, we have seen a great change in consumer habits, especially in relation to social networks. While the average time spent on social media increases, the greatest impact is how we split the time over various platforms. And TikTok is the new player who takes a bit of our social media time.

TikTok is a video application for social media to create and share short lip sync, comedy, and talented videos. Just two years old, the platform is now the world's fourth-largest and in June 2018 reaches 500 million active monthly users. And one of the most downloaded social media applications remains.

For the year 2020, social media marketers need to start looking away from the big 4 (Facebook, Instagram, LinkedIn, Twitter).

1. Building communities

The way people consume changes socially. There are five reasons. What you do as a person becomes less and more about what you can do as a community.

It is important to share ideas, to start conversations with like-minded people, to create community projects. This was seen by the major channels as they focused on groups as part of their strategy. Facebook now has more than 400 million members worldwide.

Although TikTok does not have a group element, you can see that the community is at the core of the platform. Much of the content is trend-driven, and people react creatively to the videos of others. Duets are a great example, and users can add answers for real collaboration to other videos.

TikTok offers kindergarten users the desire to avoid potential toxicity on other platforms.

2. Anti-marketing marketing

Generation Z anti-marketing does not like advertising. Fifty-one percent of them are now browsing with ad blockers. This means that the traditional SMA and SEA strategies will not work for them as well as previous generations.

You need to be less invasive instead. It is connected with this sense of community. These knowledgeable social media users are ready to engage with brands at their level. So, you are a winner when you build brand stories incorporating your community.

For this, TikTok is an ideal platform. Brands are now constructing their own channels on the platform, with content tailored to the TikTok public. That's paying off already. In September 2019, the NFL launched advertising on the platform and brought together over 541 K fans.

NFL has mastered the creation of content for the TikTok audience.

3. Content generated by users

Content generated by users will also be one of our trends for this year. And this is linked to another of these generations ' main concerns: authenticity. 90% of Millennials say that authenticity is important to them when selecting the brands to support them.

As false news has increased, consumer confidence in social media has declined in recent years. While every platform works hard to combat this issue, TikTok has the advantage of being new. As part of its design, it drives authentic content.

And this is why it focuses on UGC. It is the authentic content that is not based on marketing strategy, but on consumer advocacy–people want to talk about your brand only because they love it.

Encourage UGC whenever possible as part of your TikTok strategy. Be part of the discussion and help shape the conversation with your brand.

4. Instant, raw trend jacking

Social media is fast, raw trend jacking immediately. Trending is essential if you want to be seen as an appropriate brand and if you want to make the most of your commitment.

Speed usually costs output—but the good thing is that it no longer matters as much.

Users are more willing to forgive raw, less polished content when the trend is right.

This is not a strategy for TikTok in particular. It can work as well on Twitter, where short, sharp messages can quickly cut the sound. But TikTok has developed a raw, unfiltered content platform that you can build with minimal effort and time.

An example of fast, raw content, which was right in the trend.

5. Nano influencers

This marketing will continue to play a major role in marketing in 2020. However, expect the audience to change to disturb that too.

The people we expect are no longer influencers. Among the issues of authenticity and the rise of discerning social media users, influencers of celebrities are decreasing. The use of these large audience influencers is associated with too many risks. That and the consumers do not wish to be sold by the stars from which they are separated but turn to the smaller niche experts who have created their communities and the content they enjoy.

For TikTok, this is not just a trend. We watched this turn to microphones (up to 100 K followers) and even Nanos (up to 1000 followers) across all social media channels.

However, TikTok is ideal for nano influencers. There are no established influencers on other channels you would find. And this platform enables everyone to build a community around their content quickly and easily, offering wonderful views in a fairly short time.

TikTok – the 2020 social media disruptor

TikTok continues to be a new platform for 2020 social media disruptors. And while it has not been tried and tested, it has the potential for anyone ready to take a risk.

2020 will be the year in which the marketing of social media is disrupted, and consumer platforms other than the Big 4 will bounce. The question is, will you be there to welcome your audience on a platform like TikTok?

Chapter 3

How to Get Attention from Your Target and Get Engagement Even If They're Dumbed to Just Watch Videos

One thing you must know about how to do about your social media, particularly Tik Tok, which has to do with videos, is to draw people's attention. In this book, "Tik Tok Marketing," we'll look at what you can do to improve engagement and to get the attention of people who wouldn't normally remain after watching a video, saying they don't have time for social media. There is a very simple rule of engagement, capture them, and they will never leave you. Once this has been done, you must remain consistent with keeping things as they were, to improve each time. Let's go. Let's go.

1.   Do your own research

Research, and the acquisition of relevant information in your niche is undoubtedly the main success factor. Right into creating video and succeeding without your audience's knowledge is a great dream.

The first thing is to learn from your closest competitors, everything you can.

Know the content that they create. Learn about the specific success of such videos.

It may be difficult, but it is worth finding out that you can take calculated steps. It is by researching them that you can identify a number of gaps or errors that you can make. You can take your brand off the ground by filling the gap and doing things differently.

2. Creating useful, creative content

The ground rule is to hook the viewers while creating videos. But if you do employ two strategies, you can never hook the viewer. One of them is to churn useful videos that add value to viewers.

Another thing is an interesting thing. No one is going to give a second look at a boring take. You must remember that many spectators are looking for entertainment. You must, therefore, entertain them while passing some advertisements.

You might wonder how you get useful topics to create videos for marketing regularly. We suggest that you concentrate on success stories from people using your products or services. You can also find ways to use these products.

What is the bottom line?

Be creative and impressive.

3. Partner with Others

Although you are committed to doing your business alone, sometimes it becomes unavoidable to partner with others. You can share ideas with someone in the same industry as you. You could reveal the one thing you never did that could completely transform your traffic. You will also learn something from you that could help you. Overall, both of you are going to win here.

4. Be Consistent

It is true that a consistent supply of videos for your Tik Tok account is very demanding. It's true. This is why many companies instead prefer to run blogs. However, the good thing is that the use of marketing videos is far more effective than the writing of articles. This is because some of the videos are entertaining.

Interestingly, when it comes to entertainment, Tik Tok takes the cake. You, therefore, need to do what you need to ensure that Tik Tok videos are regularly updated. Just be consistent as if you were running a blog. It's worthwhile as you get more traffic and eventually more sales.

But this is the deal: We do not only talk about consistency in posting Tik Tok videos; we also consistently mean posting videos of quality. Inasmuch as your regular visitors have seen the quality of your videos deteriorate, they will begin to avoid you like a rattle serpent!

5. Increase the commitment of your followers (Tik Tok gives a better impression to the video)

Now here we do proper research, create useful and creative content consistently and cooperate with others. You have gained more visitors, and they are glad.

So, what's next? What's next?

If you want to bring the entire marketing to the next level, you need to improve the involvement of your followers. This will ensure that no customer can stop following your account. You can also hear from them and know what they expect from you.

I'll tell you how to reach this far precisely:

1.   Put a question video.

This is pretty straightforward.

What do you do when you have a real-life question?

Your answer. Your answer. Right? Right?

And when you answer, you feel committed. You feel that you are relevant and necessary. This also applies to Tik Tok. If you ask your fans questions, they will feel involved and loved. You will soon follow your videos faithfully, and that is the marketing you need. One rule is to ask them to regularly open-ended questions.

2.   Ask fans to make their choices

Another simple way to get your viewers involved is to offer them options. And you'll have already engaged with them when they answer. You can also get them to select their sides on some controversial life issues. Whether these problems relate to your brand or not, they will be very helpful. And when they pick, some will certainly oppose it.

In turn, this leads to a debate or discussion. If the problems are sensitive, it would be better if you didn't piss off some of your fans on any side. You can allow them to talk about themselves as you moderate and make sure they don't take them personally.

3.   Post When Your Fans Are Online

It is true that your followers have their own time when they are online. Post If your fans are online. It's also true that they love to get online for a certain time. You would preferably do your investigation and identify the time and use it. You end up getting more viewers when you post. If you post any other time, your post will be buried from the many posts of others.

4. Commitment to other brands

Another aspect that has been shown to be beneficial is to engage with other brands. It enables you to make your brand known for other ideas that you cannot reach. Some of the generated traffic will be sold. One thing you should remember here is to share content that is objective.

This is because the public watching your video from other places knows that you use it for marketing your brand. You could brush it off and make your post useless.

5. Crowdsource Feedback

You definitely need feedback from Crowdsourced to be relevant to your audience. Then you get to know whether or not they love your content. One good thing is that feedback is not a problem for people. You just have to ask for it in a good way. For example, you can't ask a friend how you performed in a public speaking contest, but they will probably applaud you so that you don't harm your sentiments.

That's what they want to do last. But if you asked them differently, exactly where you ought to improve in your next competition, then they would be quick to point out, and that is exactly where you had failed.

That's what you should do here to get honest feedback that you must continue to ask.

6.   Share Industry News and Hot Themes

Your fans make you live. They are the reason for your brand's continued success. They probably know that you promote your brand and get more money from it. You may also know you get less than you get by the end of the day.

If you take a step forward and air-curated news and thrilling topics from the industry, they know that you are also interested in their success. You want them to make informed choices. With that, they will listen to you more devotedly.

7.   Adjust your post frequency.

One important thing is your post frequency. If you post very little, a smaller audience will attract you. On the other hand, you will invest more resources and time when you post too much, while your posts go unrecognized by your audience.

What's the deal, then?

Post a small number of videos every day when most fans are online. With this, you will invest less and attract a significantly better proportion of the audience.

8.   Answer Everyone

This is straightforward. The point is that you answer every comment that you receive from your viewers. If you ignore them, they will notice you don't value them, and you end up losing your account loyalty.

9. Solicit Fan Content

It is true that you may dry up new ideas to keep your audience engaged. One way to ensure that such ideas are consistently supplied is to ask your viewers for them. You can ask them to propose subjects that they want you to cover. Or, more importantly, you might ask them to send fancy product pictures. This loyal viewer or the best picture can be rewarded.

10. Provide value

You don't want to read a straightforward article. And you don't want to watch a video that adds no value to your life. You're going to feel cheated. That's exactly how your audience feels when you share content that does not add value to their lives. They should inspire or teach them something or skill.

The bottom line: Do not upload that video if it is solely for the selling of your brand.

11. Celebrating Holidays

You can get plenty of inspiration for content to share with your fans if you can enjoy holidays and special celebrations. The deal is to adapt a certain video to what is celebrated that day. For example, you could use April's National Smiles Day to create something creative out of it.

12. Post a Quiz or Poll Video

Posting video polls, surveys, or even a simple quiz can attract certain commitments. While long surveys may seem to your audiences boring, a short test can do you good. And it could reveal something you didn't know your fans like, far from creating commitments. You can produce more videos on the linked topics from there.

13. Rethink Hashtag

Use Research has shown that posts which usually use hashtags have fewer commitments than those which do not. Hashtags are, of course, still especially good for increasing visibility. However, only for what is trending should they be used.

14. Host Contests and Giveaways

Hosting competitions and donations are sure ways to encourage commitments and attract more fans. If you regularly organize for such donations, in the long run, you will win more fans who can translate into sales. It will cost you only a little. If you give out your own products, it is even lower.

Chapter 4

How to Use Tik Tok To Drive Followers to Your Instagram And YouTube To Build Your Brand

While the concept was pioneered, Instagram has limited options to make short video stories; many users turn to other apps to create something unique. Tik Tok is an app designed solely for this purpose.

You can record and edit short videos on your smartphone to complete the experience by adding your favorite tunes. The app has almost a billion users, plus 70 million users a day. It's the perfect app to create Instagram stories that stand out from the rest.

Connect Apps and Express Yourself

You know how things work if you already use TikTok to create Instagram Stories. You may not know that you can connect both apps and make it easier than ever to create and share video in full.

With Instagram connected to TikTok, you can run the application and share your video directly to your Insta account without saving and uploading the material separately. That means you can create unique videos in minutes by sharing them directly with a single hit on your Instagram account. Your online friends will envy and wonder how you made your short videos.

If that sounds attractive, continue reading to learn how to connect both apps to your device.

Adding Your Instagram Account to Tiktok

You will need to download TikTok to your smartphone before you start if you do not already have it. Create an account, and you're ready for TikTok to add Instagram.

Tap the profile icons in the bottom right corner

- Instagram to TikTok
- Tap' Edit Profile' command
- Tap' Add Instagram '
- Open Tiktok, tap the profile icon in the bottom right corner.
- Add your Instagram to Tiktok

The Instagram login screen will take you to where your Instagram login information is requested. Once your password and username and password have been registered, tap "Login" and log in via TikTok to your Instagram account.

How to add Instagram to Tiktok

The app will then ask you whether or not you wish to remain logged in. Choose between "Save Info" and "Not Now," depending on whether or not you want to save your information with the app.

Add Instagram to Tiktok

To finalize the connection process, add Instagram to the Tiktok tap, "Allow."

TikTok is now a favorite for your Instagram account. You can now directly share your videos on Instagram without switching between applications, saving, and uploading each video separately.

Unlinking Instagram From Tiktok

If you ever wanted to un-link Tiktok from your Instagram profile, simply repeat the first two steps, tap the "Unlink" button rather than tap "Add Instagram." Then TikTok will delete your Instagram credentials as they had never been linked.

What about Linking Tiktok and Youtube?

It is also possible to link your YouTube and TikTok accounts. The process is the same as Instagram, but tap YouTube in step 3 instead of tapping Instagram. Complete the following steps, as in the example of Instagram, and your YouTube will now be linked to your TikTok.

It's much easier to share videos on Youtube because you don't have to resize or crop them at all.

How to Upload Videos from Tiktok To Instagram

The greatest difficulty people have when trying to upload a video from Tiktok to Instagram is the aspect ratio. TikTok videos are vertical and have a 9:16 aspect ratio, whereas Instagram has a maximum 4:5 aspect ratio. This means that every video has to be edited and edited before it is posted on Instagram.

Here's what to do:

First edit and save your video to your device in TikTok.

Then open your browser's Kapwing Resize Video tool. It's an online tool, so no downloads or installs are available.

Upload your video and select Instagram as your publishing platform. The tool will redimension your video to fit the recommended dimensions of the site.

To start the resize, click on the "Create" button. The process takes a couple of seconds and is done in the cloud so that your device does not crash or freeze.

Download your video in MP4 format and publish it on Instagram when all is done.

Make your videos memorable

The creation of an interesting short video in TikTok is not just about filters and effects adding. If you want your video to be viral, you will have to come up with something special.

Think of what you want to do and explore with the tools provided until you learn how it works. It'll probably take you dozens of posts before someone takes your content into consideration. Don't let it go, and you'll eventually get your Instagram fame for five minutes.

How to transform TikTok followers into YouTube subscribers

Do you want to build a TikTok fanbase but follow you to YouTube? See our tips to migrate your audience. Although TikTok does not share specific information about its users, more than 500 M people have been estimated to be active on the platform, with the largest growth in India and other parts of Asia. Did you know that in Thailand alone, the app was downloaded by 1 in 7 people!

TikTok has proven to be a fertile ground for supporters and creators, available in 75 languages, who want to build a public and a community around their content. The application has been downloaded more than 1.2 billion times, with 41% of TikTok users aged 16 to 24. This is an audience that is actively prepared for even more consumption in social media and for creators to build on it.

But while the TikTok famous youth are basking in views and followers their videos generate, there is still no way to monetize content on the app outside of third-party brand deals. While on the platform, there are ads, no ads are run on videos uploaded by creators, so there are no ways to profit from a percentage of that revenue, as with YouTube.

Of course, generating revenue via AdSense on YouTube is nowadays not a walk in the park, but designers still have the financial opportunity. But even the popular TikTok accounts have nothing like the number of subscribers that attract the top channels on YouTube, and for many TikTok uploaders, they start from scratch in the building of follow-up on YouTube. However, this can be done, and three quick tips can start:

Ways to migrate your TikTok audience to YouTube

#1 Building Upon Content You Made Popular on TikTok

While lip-syncing, or dancing around for the latest release of Arianne Grande, may have generated healthy TikTok follow-up, it won't get you to the bottom of YouTube. At all. At all. Besides the copyright-based content (which is a problem with TikTok and will lead to a download if you are caught), you can do the same old thing, but on another platform, it will get very old very quickly.

But you can build your TikTok based on your personality and quirks, and that is a fantastic start for every creator. On YouTube, watchers may come for the content, but they will stay with the creator of the content, and if you publish video content successfully elsewhere and have an understanding of what your audience likes, that is highly transferable expertise. However, you must be prepared to know what works are, which takes us to our next tip:

#2 Understanding how YouTube works

There are many similarities between TikTok and YouTube. Both are content-oriented platforms, yet like any other video creator, you will need to develop and upgrade your game significantly if you wish to succeed on YouTube. Yes, you will bring your audience to you, but to expand your subscriber base and generate the kind of views and commitment necessary to generate income on and off the platform.

Determine the purpose of your YouTube. You won't really be famous, and it's certainly not the best long-term plan. It sucks to hear, but those stars, you all remember about love, have labored for years and years—they haven't happened by accident.

It takes time, patience, and skill to understand how the YouTube algorithms work, what content to create, and how to optimize your community while growing, but when you start using the resources available on this blog and on the YouTube vidIQ channel, you're going in the right direction.

#3 Give your TikTok followers a cause to follow you on YouTube (and ask them to!)

It might be the most obvious tip worldwide, but add it into your TikTok profile when you've got a YouTube channel! If fans don't know where else you live on the internet, fans can't follow you.

Okay, now that's out of the way, consider how your TikTok audience can be encouraged to YouTube. Naturally, you can always ask them that never hurts. But also think strategically why they should follow you and offer this incentive. YouTube lets you upload 15-minute videos (longer if you are a checked channel) for this expanded content to post teasers on TikTok.

Tell your followers what to expect and be consistent on YouTube, so it becomes part of your publishing strategy. It is best practice for every creator to "create once, publish everywhere" to give your buck the maximum bang.

Chapter 5

The #1 Quality You Should Have to Have Success Here. You DON'T Have to Be A Hot Girl, Trust Me.

With the increasing preference of consumers for using online communication channels, it is important to pay attention to who is best equipped to handle such valuable relationships. Social media now includes marketing, sales, and customer service. Every manager of social media needs specific, unique skills to safeguard the digital reputation of a company.

"Looking for the best is your most important job."- Steve Jobs

Who is the best person to talk to for your company exactly?

This isn't a simple reply. After all, their work includes so many different aspects of customer visibility.

Customer experience is the sum of all brand experiences and includes the behavior, attitudes, and emotions of a customer about the brand. Savvy strategies are obligatory for navigating the nuances of each online property, and it is not a job for anybody.

Many companies are leaving their digital reputation prone to digital destruction.

It's surprising to know that many companies have not concentrated much on this position as a social media manager. Certain people have not even designate someone to manage all their online marketing components and thus make their digital reputations vulnerable.

Don't fall in the trap of thinking that your digital reputation without your attention is "just fine." Believing it is unnecessary to spend or have trouble ensuring that your reputation is safeguarded back to bite you.

It is essential to manage conversations.

Your business conversations should be monitored and administered accordingly. Someone needs to make sure that they are legitimate, informed, and a reflection of the customer experience in real life. It is risky to let this to happen with an inexperienced team or person and leads to lost sales.

If I did my job, I convinced you to employ someone to monitor your online assets. It is crucial to identify the ideal skills before you decide who this will be.

1. Savvy Social Media

She should be a regular user of social media and be well integrated into the social environment.

She/he ought to have a good story to tell. If you have a blog or write for online media, check out what you wrote. It is a great way to follow your skills and decide whether your personal brand meets the criteria of the company.

2. Branding and Marketing Experience

Social media is equal parts marketing, branding, sales, management of PR / crisis, reputation building, and data analysis.

I cannot inform you on how many individuals I met who are responsible for the social media of a company that has ZERO brandings and marketing experience.

Social media is simply a channel for engaging customers and delivering important messages that respond to their needs, concerns, and challenges. Your message and your results show the level of experience.

3. Ability to Focus

Focus capability quickly becomes an essential marketing skill. The ability to concentrate has become increasingly complex amidst the many distractions faced by social media managers.

We lost focus on social media that made art and science an interruption. The medium in which we work has given us so many distractions that it is a huge task just to keep track of what we did 15 minutes ago.

From conferences to calls to compliance training to the management of social communities, the sheer drift of interruptions is a cry for the critically acknowledged leadership.

Until then, the focus remains an individual ability to master the modern marketer.

4. Emotional maturity

A social media manager must be able to keep a perspective and, above all, not personally take things.

The ability to recognize and handle one's feelings supports the healthy online community of a brand.

Here are the signs of emotional maturity:

- when you are incorrect, you notice and verbalize (composure).
- You have created a space between sensation and reaction.
- You're pitying yourself and others.
- You know when to stop and persevere.
- You know when and how to request assistance.
- The more you understand, the less you grasp, you're all right with it.
- You're looking for self-mastery.
- You maintain a positive attitude
- You are independent
- You are true
- You are responsible
- You are accessible and gracious, and you give

5. Empathy and tolerance

Empathy is the key to great customer service, and social media IS customer service is no mistake.

The way you put yourself in the shoes of your customers helps you to understand your needs and to address them accordingly.

Intense situations of crisis, in which an audience is watched, a social media manager may not always provide a solution, but can always offer empathy.

Empathy is also essential to create high-quality social media and advertising content. Content reaches the point when the client is left thinking, "Wow, it was meant for me only!" Empathy is what enables a manager of social media to create such content.

The job of a director of social media is not easy.

Sometimes you get customers angry.

Sometimes customers need to be more careful to understand things.

Sometimes things are just going to be hard.

The worst thing you can do in such situations is to lose your coolness.

Impatience not only hinders our ability to enjoy life but makes us worse off doing difficult things (like an outstanding social media manager).

Understanding the addictive nature of wrath, irritation, and indignation helps prepare people for crises. The more people feel these emotions, the more likely they will continue to feel. Understanding this makes it clear why patience is so important.

6. Clear, concise, professional

When a company is involved, they expect (sometimes unconsciously) the correct grammar, orthography, and punctuation. It's easy to forget, so don't you.

Another buyer can expect user-generated content (the content that customers and influencers produce, such as online reviews). Prospects review reviews, and your answers to your reviews are included in their research.

Poorly written reviews or robot-sounding company speeches work against the digital reputation of a company. You can damage any goodwill that you earned, as it seems that you don't care.

7. Ability to Recognize Leads

Leads on Social media, including online review sites, are places where people share experiences and opinions. Questions often arise during these conversations.

The job of a social media manager is to recognize these issues as an opportunity for closer customers. You must distinguish a lead and treat each person as if they were physically in front of you.

Pro tip: Answer the question from your prospect and then ask another consultative question that will help them to think and sell them. These are the principles of consultative sales, but it is advocacy for the buyer.

8. A Humor Sense

Let me say that humor is not for amateurs. Social media humor is intended only for those who master it. And I mean by the master, a reasonable individual would laugh or find humor in your content.

I have included in my list here a sense of humor because you don't have to be entertaining to hold a sense of entertainment. I got lots of friends who can't say jokes or write funny posts, but they are laughing at funny things.

The shortest length of connecting between two people is Laughter.

Laughter is a universal communication medium. Humor makes a brand human. In social media (and all marketing), individuals pay big money to reduce the gap between people so that humor rules are managed successfully.

9. Industry Experience a Plus

While an additional bonus a candidate has experience in the industry of a company, it is not a requirement. An overview of activities and an immersive trek into the culture of companies will go much further.

With a high quotient of empathy, he/she will soon learn how the industry works.

10. Resolving ability–Do not inflame

The ability to balance a prompt response with a reasoned answer promotes resolution.

Inflammatory observations and behavior do no good for anyone. A social media manager can often work on its own without supervision, so a calm approach to any conversation should be available in your wheelhouse, including conflict resolution.

A manager of social media must have authority.

An empowered social media manager is responsible for and accountable for all the issues. They can scale up a problem, follow up with the involved players, and react to the customer promptly and respectfully.

They are paralyzed, and the customer receives poor service and support without authority.

Every company has to develop and implement a sensible social media strategy to manage its digital reputation and secure everything by selecting the right person with the right skills to maintain its reputation.

Part 2
The 3 Step System

Chapter 6

How to Find Your Niche on Tik Tok

You need to know how to find your niche on Tik Tok. Many creators at Tik Tok create full content in various categories and struggle to find a place within the new platform. Just as in any other social media application, you can reach a specific audience and increase your growth by choosing a laser category or' niche.'

The question, however, is, how do we find our niche, and what strategy are we using to continue to create new unique content within that niche?

The one thing that will help you consistently create ongoing content is to choose a topic you enjoy and spend hours on it. This might be a favorite show for Netflix, video games, or even a good book series. You will find that designers worldwide have created full-time jobs by filming videos of these things.

What do you like?

You probably just thought about a few things you enjoyed. What you should do now is see whether or not these things relate to one another. If they do, they can both be incorporated into your content strategy. If not, only one of these should be chosen. Turn a coin if you need it. If Tik Tok isn't just an app that is fun and you really want to build a brand and gain a mass audience, you have to laser focus. It is hard to do, especially if you love many different things and are good. You will definitely stun your growth by choosing several categories. Look at Nintendo and Buzzfeed brands. Nintendo is JUST gaming, and Buzzfeed has all the categories you can imagine. If you have the chance, check out their two social media presence. Yes, they both bring extreme revenue, as Buzzfeed is a large company with an even bigger advertising budget, which is why they have a viral type niche. Not everyone can succeed in doing this. Personal brands such as you must consolidate a niche in order to stand out and become a voice for users to keep watching.

Take Your favorite subject and come up with templates. Let's say you enjoy comedy, for example! So for your Tik Tok videos, you have to decide which content you can make with ease all the time.

- Original 15 second comedy times
- Lip syncing of comedian artists and other comedians
- Talks about new stand-up comedians you have watched live
- Filming comedy sketches
- Playing "do not laugh" challenge with friends

These are just some modest ideas that you could have done for your content.

How to Find Trending Hashtags on TikTok

In this section, we address how to find the best trending hashtags for TikTok and how you can actually make a real difference to your brand's online presence.

Why You Should Use a TikTok Hashtag Generator Tool

There are many different hashtag generator tools available, but personally, we believe that Hashtags is one of the best options for Likes.

You understand precisely what you are doing, you have good price points, you have excellent customer support, and you won't have any trouble with TikTok to use them.

Your search engine is sophisticated and advanced so that you can search for trendy hashtag options.

Once you have your extended niche ideas together and are ready to find your TikTok profile's best hashtags, jump on with Hashtags for Likes and notice how simple it is to get the most suitable hashtags for your TikTok growth plan.

Why do they matter so much?

As you can see, we've already discussed briefly why TikTok hashtags are so important. In particular, hashtags can be used for items such as labeling, information, and topics.

With TikTok, you can only put three things in the search bar when you are trying to search for relevant content, and one of these three things is hashtags.

This means that you will very likely see your content if you use a hashtag on your TikTok content that is related to what you upload, and somebody searches in the search bar.

This will give you a great chance to connect with your target audience and to follow people loyally who are genuinely enthusiastic about your TikTok profile.

- They help you find the competition: hashtags cannot only help you join with your target viewers but can also join you in the competition. This will give you a short preview of how they do things so that you can adjust your profile accordingly. This kind of exclusive information can be invaluable for the development of your own brand.
- Make your products more visible: hashtags can strengthen your brand's visibility and credibility. That is why it is also worth thinking of a hashtag that can be made directly related to your brand.
- They can increase your following by putting hashtags on photographs of your products, sharing the love with other people, and telling them about you. This has an impact, which I hope will lead to more followers.

Finding Trending TikTok Hashtags the Right Way

If you are working hard enough to find the right hashtags for your content on TikTok, this will take your brand away. Not only will you succeed in building your brand, but you will also understand your customers much better and why you are better than your competitors.

While you can think about the hashtags that your audience uses and then search for these hashtags, this is old news and mostly ineffective.

A new strategy is in the city, called expansion of the niche. Let us check what it means and how you can adapt it for the best results to your TikTok hashtag strategy.

What is the expansion of Niche?

This concept is quite new, so bear with us as we explain it. While it works to insert those hashtags into the search engine that are specifically related to your brand and use the results you achieve, there are great disadvantages.

The downside is that everyone does this and uses the results—so that everyone uses the same hashtags to grow their TikTok. Nobody is bothering to look for different hashtags or to look for more hashtags than the ones first featured. If you're set to stand out from the crowd, you really have to think about the kind of hashtags you are looking for and how basic they are compared to what you might find.

So, what's a niche expansion in this respect? An expansion of your niche is a niche closely related to your industry, in which your target group is also interested. It's not a hashtag—a concept that includes many hashtags, depending on the industry in which you are.

You sell makeup brushes, for example. But you looked up this and found only the generic hashtags—the ones that everybody else uses.

So, rather than using them, why not try looking at other niches that are similar to the maquillage brush niche, which can produce slightly less popular hashtags that can reach you more widely?

67

For instance, you could try out other niches, like' fashion artist or' model wedding,' instead of searching' makeup brush.' Hashtag quests like this are linked, niche expansion's to a' makeup brush.'

Particular TikTok hashtags similar to this are less familiar options that will not provide you with much initial information on your posts, but you will find that they are much more easily graded, so your content will be far more visible.

Then you have the effect of snowball. The more people start showing genuine interest in your content, the more they will share them—and you have a fast-growing audience before you know it.

Create Your Expanded Niche List

Certainly, one of the fundamental things you have to do while thinking of your increased niche is to pen down a number of niche choices that are closely related to your original niche but are not the same. The closer you get to the right options, the more brainstorming you do.

When you brainstorm your expanded niche ideas, other things must be thought about to make the whole process more effective.

You must also think about your target audience and also about their credentials. For example, what are they mostly gender? What is the age group in which most of them fall, and what are their typical habits and points of interest?

Finding relevant subjects for your expanded niche means learning all about your target audience and what they hope to do with your TikTok profile.

How to use the TikTok hashtags properly

There are some things to recognize before you get there and try to find the best trend hashtags for your TikTok growth to make the whole process worthwhile.

Let us look at them:

- Be captivating: when we think of your expanded niche's best hashtags, we recommend making sure they're catchy and easy to remember. We also recommend, as mentioned earlier, a specific hashtag that is either the name of your brand or is closely related to it. You can now use this brand new hashtag on all your content and spread it across your TikTok public.
- Be Simple and Effective with It: You want your target audience to be able to remember the hashtags associated with your brand easily: be simple and effective with it. You don't want to make it hard to remember them, and you definitely want to make sure you spell them right. Otherwise, you will not be able to find your target audience.
- Get trends: TikTok always rotates trends, so use your hashtag choices to try and be trending at some point to become more exposed.
- Don't be spamming: there is nothing wrong with using hashtags for you—especially because

they will go a long way to help your brand grow. However, there are too many hashtags, so we recommend that you keep the number you use nice and limited. Try to choose a few hashtags that accurately represent your brand, but we would not recommend that more than ten be used per post.

As you can see, there are some simple but effective ways to use TikTok hashtags. You can also see that we talked about the old way of searching for outdated hashtags–that means that there's a new trend. Instead of focusing entirely on your target niche, broaden your horizons and find the hashtags next to the industry. This will expand your reach and show you in a crowded market.

In conclusion, if you are serious about taking the early stages of the Tik Tok app seriously and building a brand, you must select a focus and create consistent content.

Chapter 7

How to Go Viral by Emulating Other's People Content the Right Way

TikTok is a media app for up to one minute creating and sharing short videos. This app was launched by Bytedance in 2017 for non-China markets (September 2016: Douyin for China). This application gained considerable popularity in 2018, after the fusion of musical.ly, and in October 2018 became the most used app in the US.

Nowadays, before you think about buying them, people purchase domain names (for instance, www.katyperry.com) from famous people. They benefit from your popularity and use your domain name for various purposes or sell it for thousands of dollars back to you. So now take action and book your name for your own domain.

Namecheap is the best service to register a domain name because it is secure, affordable, convenient, and offers exceptional customer support. It also offers free 2-factor authentication to prevent hackers from accessing your accounts.

What About Getting Famous On Tiktok?

Everybody likes fame, but not everyone gets it. Only those people are renowned and become famous/influential who work hard to achieve it. I've compiled this list after carefully analyzing the top influencers. Follow these rules, one day, you'll be an influencer.

Optimize Your Profile

1. Make Your Picture Stand Out

When someone first watches your video and likes it, it is likely that they will swipe over your profile to see it. The first thing he notices after swiping is your profile image. The first impression is the last. Upload an attractive profile picture and get the user's attention. You can edit your photos through any Picsart, Snapseed, and other photo editing apps.

2. Write Amazing Bio

Following a first view on the profile image; people check the organics of the account. Craft yourself in the bio section in the best way.

Use grammarly, free grammar, and orthographer to avoid errors while writing content.

Also, do not neglect to add a link to your profile to YouTube and Instagram.

Tip: Don't rely on a platform. A recent example is Mr faisu 007, an Indian TikToker who has more than 20 M TikTok followers but is now suspended. He's now uploading Instagram content, which he grew to 7 M through TikTok.

To optimize your account, you can read this blog post and switch to a professional account for free.

Some people love to dance while others love to cook. If you love both, create two accounts instead of one and post corresponding content. There are accounts that post particular niche contents rather than mixed contents. TikTok's most popular niches are dance, humor, lip-sync videos, cooking, crafts, etc.

3.   Post More Content

There is an endless debate between a few times posting high-quality content or regular content quality. I don't know which side you support. I always win (almost every time) to post more content. Posting more content allows you greater exposure and is much more likely than others to create a viral video.

4.   Create Out - Of-The-Box Stuff

Create original contents. While original content requires more effort, it also pays off. It is difficult to create original content in the early days, but you can overcome this obstacle by practice. Get used to creating five scripts every day for your videos and select the best for video creation. Your brain will usually think out of the box in a month.

5.   Participate In Challenges

Take on challenges and monitor new challenges so that you can follow them in front of others. Early videos on any challenge get as much traction as they do after millions accept it. Create the best content in your posts and use the relevant hashtags.

One of the most popular challenges was the Kiki challenge.   #bottlecapchallenge   is   becoming enormously popular nowadays.

Today, hashtags are the backbone of any social media content. Platforms use it to classify content, so don't forget to add it to your videos. In each video, add 2-3 hashtags. Don't repeatedly use the same hashtags. Sometimes you use less popular hashtags. After specific hashtags, TikTok does not support it. This piece could be attached in the future. The creation of content with hashtags will certainly increase your fan base.

6. Be Consistent

More supporters are regularly posted on social media. Create and post a specific schedule on a regular basis. Create a schedule of 8 videos a week. In one day, don't upload all the videos. Post a day or two. Sometimes you visit a good place or participate in a local event and create lots of videos. Do not upload all of them in 2-3 days at once.

7. Add A "Fimal" Travel In Your Videos

Videos with two persons perform much better than single videos. You can quickly increase your followers by toping your videos with a "female" element. Just as "Redbull gives you wings," girl gives you wings. This girl could be your sister, girlfriend, or boyfriend. Make her videos. Make some videos of girls if you disagree and check the difference.

Some videos are extremely popular; don't waste that opportunity, make similar videos, or troll them with a remake or positive criticism.

8. Recreate Popular Videos

Diversion here does not mean that you create videos outside the niche. Diversification does not mean that you create videos outside your niche. Diversification means you don't just stick to videos that synchronize lips. You can dance, add a soundtrack of your own.

Music adds soul to video.

9. Best Soundtracks

Instead of creating exceptional visual content alone, be careful to select a soundtrack. Due to the soundtrack, many average videos are popular. A recent example is the viral soundtrack of Thomas Shelby.

10. High-Quality Videos

Three ways to improve your video quality. The best equipment is used. Use high-quality cameras and lighting to produce high-quality videos.

Do the best editing of videos. Always follow trends in video editing. Use editing applications to create inviting videos. InShot, Timbre, Funimate, Vizmato are some of the best video editing apps. Neon editing nowadays is trending. You can also outsource it with Fiverr freelancers from $5. At best, dress up and always capture.

Abusive comments are common on TikTok. TikTok's abusive comments are common. If you live in a religious country, posting videos or bikini can lead to numerous abusive comments. According to the algorithm of TikTok, videos with several comments get a boost on TikTok and eventually give rise to more views, likes, and followers. If your feelings are hurt by abusive comments, turn the comments off. Otherwise, haters can bark.

An influencer is nothing without followers/fans, so interact always with them. You can interact with them by answering their observations.

You can take it to the next level by commenting on its content.

11. Hijack Attention From Other's Videos

Growth is slow in the early days. You can increase your growth by adding comments on the videos of other creators. Just follow two rules and add comments. Comment on viral videos or creators who follow a lot. Write eye-catching comments and pertinent comments.

12. Cross-Promote Your Videos

Cross-promoting is the only way to increase the folder base without creating additional content. Promote your videos across the board. It demands a lot of work to build content, so upload it to all social platforms. Upload it as the history of Instagram, post it on facebook, twitter, etc. Some TikTokers even upload their old content to TikTokby, re-uploading their previous hit videos. You can also do it.

13. Collaborate With Others

A win-win situation for all. This is a mutual way to promote one another. Always work with people with the same niche. Collaborate with others, whether you have 100 or 100 K followers. Ask people to work with similar supporters. Don't ask the 10k follower person to cooperate if you have 100.

Sunny Leone, for example, a hot Bollywood actress, is cooperating with Awez Darbar, a famous 15M+ Indian TikToker.

Positive content always brings wonderful results.

14. Create Positive Content

Some people use it beautifully to increase their commitment. You can build awareness of any environmental protection issue to support any NGO irrespective of your niche. Anyone is always admired by positive vibes.

15. Flow With Trends

Keeps an eye on the trends right now. Make content about it immediately. It can be a trending song/music, a challenge with hashtags, video play, imitation.

Tip: keep an eye on the trend section to get ideas about trending music/video. Hashtags on Twitter can also help you.

16. Ask For Feedback

Only if he/she knows where he/she is lacking can someone improve. The best way to understand your shortfalls is to ask for feedback. Ask your followers about how you can improve your lack. After receiving feedback, appreciate and work on good suggestions.

17. Go Live

Keep your audience in touch, and the best way to do this is to go live. Go live and chat with your followers very often. When you go live, TikTok notifies your followers and makes your videos more engaged.

Some followers are obsessed with creating videos with you and fulfilling their wishes by creating a video with them. These crazy fans upload content that features you and market mouths too. Finally, it will show you before a new audience.

Chapter 8

How to Create Content That Sells Your Product or Other People's Product, Even If You Don't Know Any Topic

Video has become a king of content in recent years. Companies can find new ways to pop their products, including exciting product videos, everywhere you turn.

Remember, when, as two years ago, when products had a bunch of photos, you know? These are historical days.

Videos are a great move to market your product and brand. People easily talk to video, and it evokes powerful answers. Think about how often a sweet YouTube video has teared you up, or a TV ad persuaded you to buy a product.

A survey by Animoto found that 96 percent of consumers find video helpful when shopping and, after watching a video explaining the product, 73 percent say they are more likely to buy an item. Very compelling things.

Product videos can be used in advertising on your product pages, via social media channels, and from e-mails. You give potential buyers an opportunity to take advantage of them and give them added reason to trust and accept your merchandise over others.

It was difficult to create videos without a qualified team and specialized equipment. Today, thanks to smartphones and free video editing programs, we have access to all necessary tools. Together with some time and effort, these tools can produce incredible results that will raise your store and brand to the next level.

Making product videos can be daunting, so I have prepared this guide to guide you in your first steps in the making short, simple, and snapshot videos that capture attention.

Choose a Format and Approach for Your Product Video

Before you start screaming "action," choose your product video format and approach to help you get the most out of your videos.

What's this product video going for? What is the purpose of it?

Where do you believe you will use the video you create, and who will watch it? You may have several uses for your product video, but choosing the most relevant location or platform will help shape how it is built.

Think about where your viewer will be on the customer journey. You probably don't know your brand if they watch a video on Facebook or Instagram. However, you are probably interested in your product if you are looking at your website, and you consider whether or not to buy it. So, make different ones, which appeal to the different stages instead of using the same video for ads and product pages.

Would you like to make a video specifically for publicity and sensitivity? Enhance your brand and products and be exciting. Will it be displayed on a product page? Make sure you show all the features of your item and how useful it is.

What do you want this video to look like?

Take a while to get a clear idea of what your final outcome should look like. You want to stay consistent, stick to one subject, and don't overload your video, so it feels uncomfortable.

Inspire competitors and other brands. To see what has been created, browse social media, or check websites. Engage with the ads on your Facebook or Instagram feed to show you more advertising–all of them are market research.

Have a sense of who's buying your product, how it could live, and where it can go. Videos showing certain environments or lifestyles can encourage people to buy your product. For instance, someone who purchases yoga pants may live an active lifestyle and enjoy being outside. Showing this in your ad will show how your yoga pants fit them perfectly.

What kind of video do you want?

While shooting an all-out narrative, an emotional video could be higher than your current (and mine!) skillset, decide on the style you think you can nail. Here are some quick ideas:

1. Pictures stitched together into a video

When you add music or text, the overall effect is great — a good idea for fast ads or social posts Short video looping. Like Instagram Boomerang or GIF, you can capture a few seconds with these snappy small numbers. You could even repeat the GIFs several times and create a video repeated in the same few seconds.

2. A scrolling screen capture

Record your screen while scrolling your products, remove unneeded screen parts, add some text and boom, and your ads are done.

3. Video demonstration

Show how your product looks in the real world. Perfect for product pages, they don't have to take long, but they should give customers an idea of how and any features your product looks.

4. Review Videos

These are excellent for social media and build confidence in your product and brand. Film or unbox your product yourself (or somebody else). Highlight both good and bad features (but better than bad!)–it helps to make the video credible and allows customers to choose an informed one.

5. Write down your video plan

The last thing you want is to immerse yourself in movies without a game plan. Scripting, drawing, or storyboarding the plan for your video is an intelligent move to make sure you are able to prepare the images properly. If you don't, at least have a strong idea of what you want to look like the finished product.

You should also decide where your video and product fit into, taking things such as lighting and the ease of filming in this particular place into consideration.

Some simple video ideas may be the floor, a table, or against a wall for the first time. Try a crosswalk, a lively street, or a metro terminal for a more urban look. And when you want an outdoor atmosphere, go to the local park, your own backyard or a local lake or beach.

While the configuration is important, avoid any distractions from your product. The last thing you want is that lovely dog in the park who steals the show.

Quick tips: Use a tripod. Quick tips keep your shots with a tripod and look professional. If at least you don't find a way to stabilize your camera so that there's no motion (I used a book stack).

Don't use the zoom feature of your phone. Phone cameras tend to use a digital zoom that is grainy. Just move closer instead to keep your shots tight.

Think vertically before shooting. Usually, you should try and film your video –your video can always be edited later, but vertical filming cannot be undone. However, if vertical pictures or images are what your video demands, go for them.

Be aware of lighting. You don't have to have fancy light for shooting a video, but don't take a look at the sun or at a bright window, because your subject is a silhouette. Try filming your subjects in front of the light source instead.

Use a microphone or second phone to include audio. Instead of using a phone for film and audio recording, set up a microphone and a second phone closer to your topics to capture high-quality sound. During editing, sync the audio and visual together.

Choose your editing software

1.   GoPro Quik app or editing software

You have a bunch of pictures and videos now. All of them must be put into a single video. Fortunately, there are many free and easy-to-use video editing programs and applications to assist you. Try finding a program with tutorials online if you're new to editing so you can find help if you get stuck.

Some of them work depending on what you are editing:

2.   Mobile: Quik

Made by GoPro, this free app takes videos and pictures from your phone gallery and edits them automatically in a video-perfect when you need a video quickly. It also allows you to edit what is created manually so that you can be sure it matches your look.

3.   Mac: iMovie

Free for all Mac users, iMovie makes things easy for beginner publishers. Moreover, there are plenty of tutorials for iMovie online to help you get stuck.

4.   Windows / Linux / Mac: OpenShot

This open-source editor is free for any operating system. It's easy to use, but still powerful enough to produce high-quality videos.

Example 1: Simple Video Ad

Editing a product video in Imovie

I decided to create a simple ad from Instagram Story for a cat-shaped look. I wanted to make the video in the way I saw other brands, edit several images in a video together, and set it to pop-y music.

I planed the pictures I wanted to use first. Instagram Story ads could last up to 15 seconds—I don't want my ads to last that long, but I wanted to know that I had sufficient potential images.

I wanted photos to show my product, the colors, and how it looked when worn. I have also decided to include a few good-measure photos of cats because I didn't have a cat model on hand. I chose some free stock pictures for cat watches. This is a fabulous tool that lets you use music without a license. If you download a song on BenSound, the terms of use for the song are specified.

I began editing the video using iMovie and imported the audio and 13 of the best photos I took, plus the cats and a Canva title card. I cut the length of the picture to try to fit the beat of the music—for most of 0.5 seconds.

At the end of the video, I added a title card, so the brand name and logo are the last things viewers can see. Since this video is for Instagram Stories, the brand name and logo will appear in the upper left corner, so I have decided to do no other thing except for the last frame.

After the finished iMovie video was downloaded, I used Kapwing to resize the Instagram Stories video (although in the YouTube version below, you cannot tell that).

Here is the ultimate result:

Nothing is fancy and more polished, but it shows my product, it's a little fun, and it doesn't take long to make it. In all, it took around an hour and a half to create the video from start to finish, and this included watching a few tutorials for iMovie.

Example 2: Designing a product video

Adding a video to a product page is an excellent way of presenting your product and giving potential customers the best opportunity to see how it looks in real life. Because of this, I needed to attach a fanny pack store video to my product pages.

I was thinking about what a customer looking at this video wanted to know and settle on a video that shows somebody interacting with the bag. I wanted to show the fanny pack features, its versatility, and size. The video would back up my description of my written product directly over the video on the page.

I wanted to do this in a light, bright environment when I shot my video. I set up a camera with a white wall and simultaneously filmed all the images to keep the video constant.

Imovie editing product video footage

Because I wanted the video to be the final decision maker for purchasers, it was important that it informed them about the product quickly and was not taken out. When editing, I made sure that I used images that showed the product features and reduced the excess. I kept some sections regularly but made others faster, so the video was not too long.

I also added details I wanted to highlight in title cards. iMovie allowed me to include text with title cards, but I was unable to find a way to insert my logo. I made it in Google Slides instead, took a screenshot, and inserted it as pictures into the video. Hey, you have to get creative sometimes and find a workaround.

This time, I chose music that I didn't think would detract from the video or turn buyers off, unlike Instagram.

Check out this finished product:

Again, I'm unlikely to win an Academy Award anytime soon, but it's still a video that meets my needs. It shows clearly what the bag looks like, how it looks, and how it looks when worn differently—all the details that customers wish to know.

You have it as a guide to film your own product videos for your brand. Start filming your own product videos.

Do you feel inspired? Good—this is your turn now!

5. Go out and start to film

Do not be dismayed if it takes time to find what works or editing is difficult, all these things will improve in practice.

Indeed, if you're like me, a couple of attempts might have failed before the final product, but this is all part of the creative process.

TikTok FAQs

Most Frequently Asked Questions and Answers□

Q) Where is the TikTok app developed?

A) TikTok was created in China, which was purchased in November 2017 from a Chinese company, ByteDance.

Q) What is TikTok's feature for users?

A) The social platform for music and video sharing enables users to create lip sync videos on their favorite songs, with built-in videos and social media platforms.

Q) Does TikTok differ from Musical.ly?

A) These two applications were essentially the same and used to provide the same function and features.

Q) Is TikTok and Musical.ly identical?

A) Both apps created by different developers were previously different. But after ByteDance got Musiacl.ly this year, the two apps were combined and will now be called TikTok.

Q) What is going to happen to exist users of Musical.ly?

A) There is no need to worry about existing Musical.ly users because they will be moved with their content and folders to the TikTok platform and will enjoy all the features and functions as before.

Q) Can I create TikTok dance videos?

A. Yes, while you lip-sync and groove your dance steps into your favorite song or music tone, you can easily create dance videos.

Q) Are both Android and iPhone available?

A) Yes, this app is available for download from both popular mobile platforms.

Q) How can I download TikTok to my device and install it?

A) On your device, you just have to open your app store, search and download and install TikTok, just like other applications.

Q) How do I register with TikTok?

A) You can easily and quickly create your profile on TikTok by registering either with your phone number or email address.

Q) Can I watch other users ' clips and videos?

A) Yes, user profiles are public by default, and you can see their creations by searching by name and genre or by feeds.

Q) Can I create my video personally?

A) You can easily create and edit clips using a number of effects and other features with a variety of features and special effects provided by TikTok.

Q) Can I restrict my videos to other people?

A) TikTok profiles are public by default, but you can change it by confidentiality.

Q) What privacy configurations do TikTok offer for video viewing?

A) There are currently only two configurations available, Private—you can only view your videos or Public—everyone can view your videos on the app.

Q) Can I use my videos with Emojis?

A) Yes, TikTok offers users so much with 100 + Emojis and face filters and beauty effects.

Q) How can I control the views of my kids on TikTok?

A) You can check the appearance of improper content using a special feature designated Digital Wellbeing.

Q) Can I limit my TikTok time?

A) You can also enable Digital Wellness and limit your app time.

Q) How do I record my TikTok dance video if it's somewhat dark?

A) Within the app, you can activate the Flashlight feature via the settings.

Q) How do I build a duet on TikTok with someone far from me?

A) You can use the duet feature in the following steps: Select your friend's video, but it must be under 15 seconds.

Tap Start a duet by selecting on the video page.

Q) How can I save my created video?

A) Just tap the video, go to the bottom right corner, and select and tap Save.

Q) How do I remove a video?

A) Tap the video you want to delete, move to the bottom right corner and select and tap to delete it. You can currently only delete individually and not in bulk.

Therefore, it is time to present the music star in your company with all your questions and start creating and sharing interesting videos.

Glossary

"Profile"

This is what you create, which is unique to you. You only need an e-mail address or a telephone number to create a profile on TikTok. You will also have to enter your birth date. It's up to you to customize your profile by adding a photo or a name for the display (this is separate to your username) and how much you want to customize your profile.

"Community"

Our TikTok users build a community and come together to create, share, and inspire. This community is key to TikTok and the individual contribution of each user to the platform. We encourage and encourage positive and respectful conduct among our members. Our Community Guidelines are there to be followed and to ensure confidence and respect are maintained in the entire community. There is no room in the TikTok community for harmful or dangerous content, violence, discrimination or hate speech, abuse or sexual activity, harassment or cyberbullying, and erroneous content. TikTok advocates the safety and intellectual property of its users.

"Creators"

TikTok users are called creators because they contribute to the shaping of the community's immersive experiences. They truly create content and their experiences, which is why we call them' creators!' They produce unique short videos shared with the community of TikTok that are special moments, experiences, or impressions of the day. They demonstrate their creativity with music, dance, sport, funny sketches, and more. The chances are endless.

"Fans"

If you're excited about another user's content, you can become a' fan' and follow their profile to ensure you don't miss any of their activities!

"Hearts"

By clicking on the heart on the right of the screen, you can show your admiration for a video. Clicking the heart auto-generates a collection of your favorite videos within your own profile, so you can view them later.

"Comments"

You can leave comments on videos of other people. In order to give our designers complete control and to ensure that these conversations remain constructive and inspiring, users can filter comments through keywords of their choice or disable them.

"Private Messaging"

You can speak to another user and exchange content privately via the Private Messaging function. Like other parts of the app, you control who chats with you— and who doesn't. View these privacy and security settings permissions.

"For you feed"

The' For you feed' feed is available from your homepage and is where new videos on the basis of users, creators, and videos that you already want are recommended to you. Do not forget to look for awesome new creators that you will love.

"Duets"

This is a feature that allows a creator to work with a different video user. More about Duets can be found here. You can only duet with somebody with their respective creator's permission. Everyone has full control over who can play duets on their videos with them. Visit privacy and security settings to modify these permissions.

"Reactions"

This is another function that allows users to react to videos that show how they feel, whether they are amazed, moved, or entertained. Like Duets, this function requires permission from users.

"Report"

This is a feature that helps maintain a positive TikTok community. We are concerned about your safety, which is why the moderators of TikTok are here to ensure that everybody complies with our Community guidelines. Users are urged to report user profiles, videos, chats, and content that include harassment, offensive behavior/comments, or unsatisfactory content. This is intended in conjunction with the Community guidelines to ensure the safety of users.

"Digital Wellness"

This is another feature that helps us maintain our users ' well-being. The new "Digital Wellness" feature allows you to manage screen time in a restricted mode. You can limit your application to 40, 60, 90, or 120 minutes per day. If you have reached the time limit, you must have a passcode to remove the setting. When enabled, the restricted mode tries to ensure that inadequate content is filtered from the user feed For You.

Made in the USA
Coppell, TX
13 December 2021